Cryptocurrency

Learn Cryptocurrency Technology Quickly

What you need to know in an hour

By

Daniel Reed

© **Copyright 2017 by Daniel Reed - All rights reserved.**

This document is geared towards providing exact and reliable information in regards to the topic and issue covered. The publication is sold with the idea that the publisher is not required to render accounting, officially permitted, or otherwise, qualified services. If advice is necessary, legal or professional, a practiced individual in the profession should be ordered.

- From a Declaration of Principles which was accepted and approved equally by a Committee of the American Bar Association and a Committee of Publishers and Associations.

In no way is it legal to reproduce, duplicate, or transmit any part of this document in either electronic means or in printed format. Recording of this publication is strictly prohibited and any storage of this document is not allowed unless with written permission from the publisher. All rights reserved.

The information provided herein is stated to be truthful and consistent, in that any liability, in terms of inattention or otherwise, by any usage or abuse of any policies, processes, or directions contained within is the solitary and utter responsibility of the recipient reader. Under no circumstances will any legal responsibility or blame be held against the publisher for any reparation, damages, or monetary loss due to the information herein, either directly or indirectly.

Respective authors own all copyrights not held by the publisher.

The information herein is offered for informational purposes solely, and is universal as so. The presentation of the information is without contract or any type of guarantee assurance.

The trademarks that are used are without any consent, and the publication of the trademark is without permission or backing by the trademark owner. All trademarks and brands within this book are for clarifying purposes only and are the owned by the owners themselves, not affiliated with this document.

Table of Contents

Introduction 1

Part I: What Is Cryptocurrency 3

    Chapter 1: The Rise Of Cryptocurrencies 4

    Chapter 2: Cryptocurrencies Vs. Currency 7

Part II: The Cryptocurrency Mechanisms 14

    Chapter 3: Cryptocurrency Functions And Components 15

    Chapter 4: Starting A Cryptocurrency Transaction 21

    Chapter 5: Blockchains And Mining – The Key To Cryptocurrency 32

    Chapter 6: Putting It All Together – Mining, Buying And Selling With Cryptocurrency 39

    Chapter 7: Getting Cryptocurrencies – Wallets And Exchanges 43

    Chapter 8: The Future Of Cryptocurrency 50

Conclusion 53

Preview Of ' Blockchain–Learn Blockchain Quickly. What You Need To Know In An Hour' 56

Introduction

I want to thank you and congratulate you for purchasing this book, "Cryptocurrency - Learn Cryptocurrency Technology Quickly. What you need to know in an hour." This book will talk about cryptocurrencies in plain language, without a minimum of extensive technical jargon, so that you can understand in a very short period, what the fuss about cryptocurrency is all about.

Understanding cryptocurrency is important if you are serious about getting the full grasp of how the internet and computer technology is affecting and will affect, our lives. Cryptocurrency as a medium of exchange, is becoming increasingly popular and may just replace many forms of payment that we have today. You do not want to wake up one morning and wonder where the world went.

It is important to know that this will be a book about cryptocurrency and *not* Bitcoin. While Bitcoin is the most popular form of cryptocurrency, it is not the only cryptocurrency in use today. Contrast that before January 3, 2009, when the first units of Bitcoin were issued, there were other attempts at a mass form cryptocurrency, which did not catch on, until Bitcoin, or the programmers behind Bitcoin, solved the problems that plagued those previous versions.

As of the end of June 2017, there were about 900 cryptocurrencies "in circulation" including Bitcoin. In less than nine years since Bitcoin was "minted," several cryptocurrencies such as Ethereum and Litecoin surfaced. So while Bitcoin is a cryptocurrency, cryptocurrency is not Bitcoin.

Part I of the book will introduce you to the concept of cryptocurrency, why it came about, and how it is created. This part will give you an appreciation of how many people felt that there was an urgent demand for a new way to pay for goods and services that circumvents traditional central banking systems of sovereign countries.

In Part II, we will discuss the heart and soul of cryptocurrency – the cryptographic systems and how its millions of users contribute how it is operated and maintained. The key concepts of blockchains, exchanges, and wallets are discussed to give you a clearer idea of their roles in the world of cryptocurrency. I will then discuss the various ways that they can be obtained and kept.

After reading this book I trust that you will have a solid enough understanding cryptocurrency to encourage you to obtain a more in-depth understanding of its workings, benefits, and dangers. Like any other financial instrument or product, there are always precautions that you need to take before you use your hard-earned money.

I hope you enjoy it!

Part I

What is Cryptocurrency

Chapter 1

The Rise of Cryptocurrencies

On a cool balmy Sunday afternoon on September 14, 2008, executives of Bank of America and the British bank Barclays had some bad news for Richard "Dick" Severin Fuld Jr., Chairman of Lehman Brothers, the giant Wall Street investment bank. They informed a sullen Fuld that they were pulling out of talks to save Fuld's once esteemed institution – there just wasn't enough money, assets, and shareholder support to prop it up. It was a conclusion that seemed unimaginable - Lehman Brothers founded in 1870, was considered one of the most stable financial institutions in the world.

The next day, Lehman Brothers announced that they were filing for bankruptcy protection – which began the process of its eventual liquidation. Lehman was the biggest institutional bust in the 2008 worldwide financial crises, which led to trillions of dollars in losses for everyone; individuals and companies; big or small. The Dow Jones Industrial Average lost over 500 points during the day, wiping out billions in public and private wealth.

About a month later, a shadowy recluse named Satoshi Nakamoto published a paper on The Cryptography Mailing list at **http://www.metzdowd.com/mailman/listinfo/cryptography** describing what he termed a new digital currency. Less than three months after releasing the paper, "Bitcoin: A Peer-to-Peer Electronic Cash System," Nakamoto released the initial digital currency software and issued the first units of the new cryptocurrency which he called Bitcoin.

Many asserted that the timing of Nakamoto's release of this software and the issuance of the first bitcoins were a response to the financial meltdown. Others argued that the while timing was just a coincidence, it seemed that the world had lost its trust in not only the financial institutions that precipitated the crises, but also in the governments that were supposed to be the watchdogs to prevent exactly what happened in the 2008 meltdown.

Apart from the massive monetary and assets losses, the biggest loss during the crisis was the loss of trust by people in their long revered and respected institutions. In the blink of an eye, the assets of many Americans sank under the groaning weight of unsustainable debt. Mortgage debt greatly exceeded the values of their houses, stock losses ravaged their retirement funds, and as companies closed down, loss of incomes created a vicious cycle of financial and economic desperation. But perhaps the most chilling aftermath of the crises was what happened to "basic" money.

For investors, the closest thing to putting currency under the mattress was investing in money market funds. These funds are where businesses "park" their overnight cash, and while it earns practically nothing in terms of interest, it is at the very minimum, supposed to retain its value. However, on Wednesday, September 17, the world woke up to find out that these funds had lost almost $150 billion on the aggregate. Going back to the mattress analogy, it was like waking up and finding out that the $100 that you had the night before was now just $99, which meant that someone had "stolen" money from your otherwise safe mattress.

The U.S. dollar, the most stable and reliable store of value, was on the brink of collapse, and the world of money and currencies as the world knew it, seemed like it was teetering on the verge of collapse.

Some people like Satoshi Nakamoto while feeling betrayed, did not take things lying down. Instead of sulking and regretting personal financial losses, they began working hard for a new stable monetary world.

Chapter 2

Cryptocurrencies vs. Currency

<u>Currency</u>

Before I describe what cryptocurrency is, it would be useful to quickly describe what that dollar bill in your pocket is, or currency. Currency is a paper, metal, or electronic representation of a "medium of exchange" which facilitates the exchange of goods and services between parties. Currency by itself (paper or metal) has little or no value, especially in its electronic form, when you pay someone online through your bank phone app or website, for example.

Currency's value comes the fact that it was issued by a national government, for example, the United States, which guarantees its face value after it prints the money and distributes it to the public. Governments in this case are "Trusted Parties," acting as a middleman in facilitating this exchange.

Currency can also be transferred and paid on the internet. You can transfer money or pay for bills using the internet, or some third-party payment or remittance service like Western Union. A few strokes on a keyboard are all that's required. You can also pay through credit and debit cards, transferring electronic currency from our deposit accounts to these cards.

This sounds like a great arrangement, and it usually is. For more or less stable governments like the United States and most Western European countries, the U.S. dollar and the

Euro are "trusted" stable currencies, and no one would think twice taking them as the form or payment for anything.

Now consider two scenarios where the typical currency model might fall apart. There are many countries whose governments are not quite as stable or reliable, at least from a currency standpoint unlike than the U.S. or countries the European Economic Community, which share the Euro. These governments have unstable political structures and are be run by despots and irresponsible officials who either use their country's treasury as the personal wallet, or have no idea how to manage their countries' finances including their currency. The worst thing they can do aside from stealing the money is to print so much of it that the value of the money drops like a rock, because of so-called "hyperinflation."

For example, imagine that you go to sleep planning to spend $10 to buy a gallon of milk, a loaf of bread, and a can of SPAM the very next morning. When you go to the grocery the next day, you are told that all your $10 can buy now is a stick of gum. The government that you trusted has just suddenly reduced your purchasing power and diminished your lifestyle! This is what happened for example, in Zimbabwe under President Robert Mugabe in 2007-2008, where prices doubled every 24 hours for several days.

Or consider a woman in an impoverished country like Afghanistan, who was using a bank branch in the capital Kabul to withdraw cash and pay for her groceries. But a suicide bomber blew himself and five others on August 29, 2017, removing her only source of money. In a flash lost the ability to use currency to pay for her necessities.

In these cases, the "Trusted Parties" of Zimbabwe and Afghanistan could not guarantee the safety and access of their citizens' money. When the value of money falls below what it is expected to be or you cannot get to your money at all, a safer and more convenient alternative is both needed and required.

There are also hundreds of millions of people that live in "underbanked" and unbanked countries worldwide, where there are no current banking or currency systems to facilitate commerce. In the United States, we take it for granted that we have bank accounts and access to spending power whenever we need it. However, the story is different in many places around the world. Africa is a glaring example where some countries unbanked population represents up to 90% of their population.

Enter cryptocurrency.

Cryptocurrency

The best way to define cryptocurrency is by describing its features. While it is still a medium of exchange in the currency sense of the word, it possesses very different qualities from the currencies that we have been used to.

First, the "crypto" in cryptocurrency comes from the word cryptography, which is simply, writing and interpreting code. Cryptocurrency was and is created by creating computer code and assigning ownership and value to this code. *Like any other currency*, paper or otherwise, it has "value" because people assign it value and more importantly, people THINK that it has value, despite the fact that all it is is a bunch of zeros and ones digitally assembled into monetary values.

The first major cryptocurrency, Bitcoin, was created in 2009 by a series of complex mathematical formulae that were run on computers with at the time, possessed significant processing power. Because it apparently removed the shortcomings of other attempts at creating cryptocurrency in prior years, its value was established as legitimate. People added value to it because they started to believe that like paper money, it could be used as a common medium of exchange for goods and services.

Second, because of cryptographic sequences and processes, it is not possible to duplicate a cryptocurrency unit once it is "created". This is like the serial numbers on a dollar bill, except that dollar bills, like all paper currencies, can be counterfeited or duplicated. A $100 U.S. dollar bill with a serial number of K01134564H for example, can be forged and "used again" depending on how many times it can be illegally copied.

This is not possible with cryptocurrency, because of multi-ledger approach, coding and mathematical probabilities, which will all be discussed later, make it impossible to do so. This prevents what is called, "double spending," an undesirable situation which is equivalent to using counterfeit paper currency.

Third, an important aspect for most cryptocurrency is that there is a limited number of unites that will be produced. Nakamoto, the Bitcoin founder, set a cap on how much Bitcoin can ever be generated, 21 million, until the year 2140. After this date, no more new Bitcoin will be created. This is expected to add to the value of the cryptocurrency, because unlike currencies issued by national governments, there is no printing press that can create currency on a whim.

Fourth, there is no single "Trusted Party" in a cryptocurrency network like a central bank in a national government maintaining a national currency. Because a decentralized system of verification, coding, transaction recording, and ledger keeping depends on the consensus of hundreds of thousands, and maybe millions of cryptocurrency miners and coders, a cryptocurrency system's trustworthiness is probably unassailable.

An increasing band of people, most of which do not know each other, verify and validate the mathematical algorithms that are the backbone of a cryptocurrency system. Cryptocurrency software is "open-source"; nobody owns or controls it, and its design is public. More importantly, everyone who wants to take part in its operation can play a role in its operation.

This "openness" can also be considered a weakness by critics of the cryptocurrency system because since there is no central authority governing the issuance and use of the currency, there is also no fallback in case of theft, dishonesty, or losses arising from cryptocurrency transactions.

Still Nakamoto and his minions have apparently found the answer to having a reliable currency, which ironically does not rely on trusting any single person or persons.

Creating money – currency vs. cryptocurrency

As with any other currency created by a national government, there are two major aspects of managing and transacting in, the currency. The first is how the currency is made, and the second is how the currency is used. With the U.S. dollar, there are really two kinds of money – money in the form or coins and paper which we are most familiar with, and money in the form of bank deposits.

In creating deposits, the U.S. government "creates" money by selling government securities such as Treasury bonds and Treasury bills, and depositing funds to the banks' accounts. The banks, using a fraction of money deposited by their depositors as "collateral," lend money to individuals and companies, make investments, which increase the money supply in the economy. A portion of this, about 10% is issued in the form of paper currency and coins which only the U.S. Treasury can print out. Banks "buy" this physical currency from the U.S Treasury and in turn, issue them to the public.

With cryptocurrency, there is no central banking authority that issues any new funds or currency for spending by the general public. There are also no "middle men" such as banks who will facilitate the creation and distribution of the new currency. Cryptocurrency is created through the interaction of thousands, and perhaps millions of cryptocurrency "miners" who try to solve mathematical puzzles and formulae devised by a particular cryptocurrency's founders and software designers.

Using money – currency vs. cryptocurrency

There are two ways that currency can be used as a medium of exchange. The first and most common worldwide, is using physical coinage and paper money. The other is using electronic and digital means to use the money to transfer money balances from one account to another. In electronic transfers, there could be at least two more parties in a payment transaction aside from the payer and the payee. For example, look what happens when Alice has to use her bank to pay Bob $100 by transferring money to his bank:

Andy→ $100 →Andy's Bank →$100 →Brenda's Bank → $100 →Brenda

<-- SUPERVISED BY CENTRAL BANKING SYSTEM -->

Somewhere along the way, either banks will collect a fee for the payment transaction. When Alice pays via credit card, there are also at least two more additional parties in the transaction: the credit card company and the bank that processes Alice's credit card. In this case, Bob will pay a transaction fee for the privilege of getting paid by Alice's credit card.

In a regular currency system, Alice and Bob rely on two or more external parties and on these external parties' systems. They assume that the banks and other intermediaries that handle their financial transactions are financially sound and honest. After 2008 and Lehman Brothers, this assumption was shaken at its very foundation.

In a cryptocurrency system, the payment from Andy to Brenda is direct, just passing through the cryptocurrency's mathematical algorithm network:

Andy→ $100 → MATH ALGORITHMS→ $100 →Brenda

The independence from a centralized authority while an attractive feature of cryptocurrency is also its biggest drawback. There is no authority or central agency to go to when a problem arises. For example, some units of Bitcoin have been observed and reported to have just disappeared into thin air in the early days of Bitcoin's operation. There is no currently no mechanism yet available to address, much less fix, transaction problems that may arise from cryptocurrency transactions.

Part II

The Cryptocurrency Mechanisms

Chapter 3

Cryptocurrency Functions and Components

At its core, CRTC is simply a digital file that lists various accounts and money just as a physical ledger would. A copy of this file exists on every node in the CRTC network. Note that if you are just sending and receiving money, or buying ro selling using CRTC, you do have to maintain or monitor any ledger in the CRTC system. A person does not have to maintain a ledger just to use Bitcoin to send and receive money, this is for people who want to help maintain, and obtain "compensation" from the system.

In typical currency and monetary systems, the functions of currency creation, distribution, monitoring, and protection are vested in separate organizations, all of them under the watchful eye of regulators. In the United States, this would include the U.S. Treasury, the Federal Reserve, and the Federal Deposit Insurance Corporation, which insures bank deposits up to a certain amount. Under this umbrella are the individual banks, the credit card companies, and other various independent financial intermediaries such as Western Union, Xoom, and small neighborhood check cashing places.

In its own way, the currency system has been "decentralized" whereby you can pay for groceries at your supermarket check-out counter by swiping your card and make purchases online. The controls, custody, and processing of payments however, are still in the hands of the centralized powers.

In a cryptocurrency system, all the functions we described previously are carried out by a huge and growing network of users with a cryptocurrency system. While some enterprising entities have come up with ways to facilitate their processing, such as wallet and exchange systems, the functionality is still dependent on how this network of users behave in the aggregate. For the most part, in its less than ten years of existence up to this writing, the major cryptocurrency systems have worked with impressive reliability with very few glitches and problems.

All the functions of cryptocurrency creation, distribution, and acquisition are performed within that cryptocurrency's basic programming rules and the actions of its users. All of the users work in tandem and mostly in cooperation, to ensure that the cryptocurrency network functions properly. The discussions of various mechanisms in the following chapters, while appearing to be in some form of chronological order, are in fact, part of a system where the parts are all working the same time: cryptocurrency creation, acquisition, payments, transfers, and recording. In our "real world" where we are interested mostly in using cryptocurrency as money, the things that we will be mostly concerned about are wallets with their transaction keys; the transactions that travel across, and populate the network; miners, and of course, the consensus blockchain, the "ledger" linking that controls the system, and is the heart and soul of cryptocurrency systems.

The shows the various functions and features that are part of a cryptocurrency system. Before we dive into how transactions are processed, let us discuss the various parts of the cryptocurrency ecosystem.

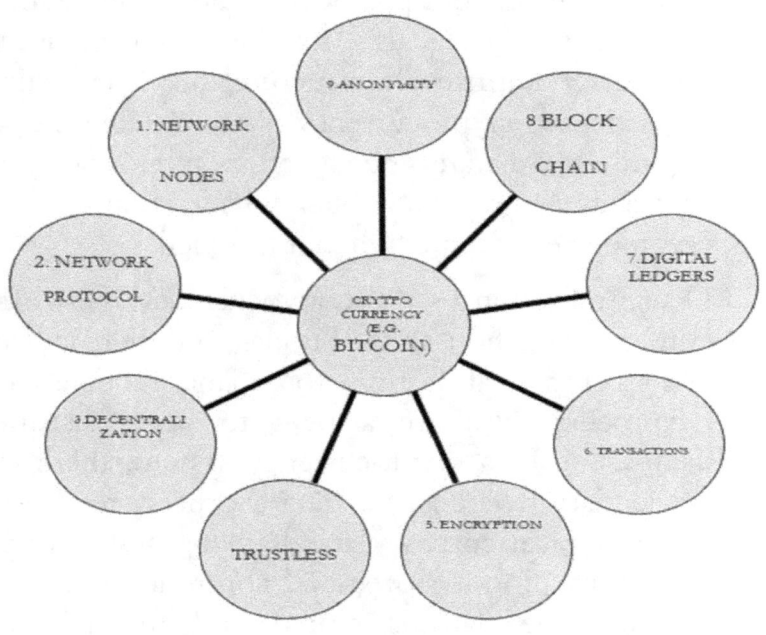

The Cryptocurrency Processing Network

1. Network nodes – A cryptocurrency system is comprised of a wide web of independent but cooperative "nodes" of users who comprise the buyers, sellers, and miners (those who work to get "newly issued" cryptocurrency units). Depending on the cryptocurrency (Bitcoin, Litecoin, Ethereum, etc.) these nodes, which represent individual consumer users can be in the tens of thousands.

2. Network protocol – This is the original "system" that was designed by the founders, creators, or inventors of a particular cryptocurrency. In Bitcoin's case, it is Satoshi Nakamoto and his (presumed) collaborators. It represents the rules, mechanisms, and code that runs the cryptocurrency. If you were building a road

system, the network protocol would be the roads, the signage, and the signals. It is the basic programming code that comprises the structure and functionality of a particular cryptocurrency system. The network algorithms dictate how transactions flow, and especially how to obtain new units of the cryptocurrency if and when it is issued.

3. Decentralization – A cryptocurrency network is comprised of thousands of nodes, and there is also no one central authority to manage data flow. Cryptocurrencies are a peer to peer, distributed database – In a cryptocurrency system, there is no single place where all the data for the system resides. Unlike typical currency and banking systems where the information is stored and controlled in a central location, the data is stored and maintained by thousands of parties working within the system.

4. Trustless - The big problem with centralized banking institutions was, as the 2008 financial crises showed, that they could not be trusted. Satoshi Nakamoto wanted a system that required no trust in anyone, much less a centralized one. The computing problem that tried to solve was the so-called Byzantine Emperor's Problem, where you needed a system of numerous redundant checks and balances to make sure that all the transactions in the system are accurate and not subject to error or fraud. The blockchain system provides this system of checks and balances.

5. Encryption – Mathematical encryption is the basis of the trustless function. All transactions within the system are subject to heavy encryption and this is one of the attractions of a cryptocurrency protocol.

Transactions are processed and approved using an approach where it is statistically impossible to introduce corrupt data, create duplicate information, and "steal" information. Together with the large distributed database, the encryption algorithms differentiate the system's security from others that need heavy security features.

6. Transactions – Consists of the transfer of funds between two parties. In a cryptocurrency system, this transfer is made between two or more digital "wallets" which house the currency. The other "transaction" that happens within the system is mining, where system members are able to obtain new cryptocurrency by solving complex mathematical and cryptographic puzzles.

7. Digital ledgers – This is where all the information of a specific transaction takes place. Each transaction and each ledger are singularly unique based on the encryption system, and these ledgers are available for everyone on the network to see, a feature that allows transactions to be verified and approved by the network of users. These ledgers are called public ledgers, because they need to be made available to all parties within the system.

8. Blockchain – This is at the same time the most important component and the most important function of a cryptocurrency system. It incorporates the trustless and encryption functions to facilitate the recording and verifying of cryptocurrency transactions. It allows the nodes to agree at regular intervals on the true state of transactions in a ledger. Blockchains comprise the unshakeable and solid

foundation of the major cryptocurrency systems like Bitcoin. The blockchain has captured the attention of the computing world since Satoshi Nakamoto released his new currency, Bitcoin, in 2009. Many have called it the fifth evolution of computing because it has supposedly created the crucial missing "trust layer" on the internet.

9. Anonymity – The true identity of the founder (founders?) of Bitcoin, Satoshi Nakamoto has never been revealed, nor does it look like it will never be. Anonymity is a pervading principle around a cryptocurrency network. Hashes and public and private keys, which we will be discussing shortly, replaces specific identifiers such as names and account numbers within the network, unless someone wants their true identity revealed.

Chapter 4:

Starting a Cryptocurrency Transaction

Before we go with the detailed discussion of a cryptocurrency transaction, let us have a high-level look at the cryptocurrency system. At its very core, the cryptocurrency ledger just lists accounts and money like a regular bank ledger. The big difference is that this file exists on every node or computer on the network. For example, a ledger like the following will exist in every node:

LEDGER	
Andy	6.5
Brenda	7.25
Cal	.50
Denise	4.4
Edward	100
Fran	65.0

This ledger exists on each and every node in the cryptocurrency in the world:

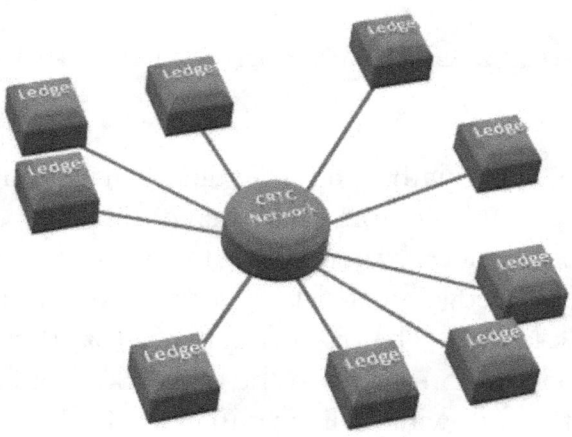

The numbers in the ledgers really do not represent anything physical in the financial world outside of the cryptocurrency system. They have value because the users have decided that they have value, and that they can use the currency to buy and sell real world goods and services. The United States Federal Reserve "created" U.S. currency many years ago, and let people believe that the paper and money and coins that they created were worth money (initially because of gold backing). The world of cryptocurrency has created the same faith and belief.

The figures and information in the ledgers possess value because the participants in the system believe that they digital currency has value. While the Federal Reserve has given us faith that we can trust the system to use the currency circulating around the world, in the digital world of cryptocurrency, the transaction histories represented in the ledger IS THE CURRENCY.

Detailed Sample Transaction

Let us begin our journey into the guts of cryptocurrency with a very simple example of how a cryptocurrency transaction works in real life by using a simple buy and sell transaction. For simplification purposes, we will use the abbreviation "CRTC" to represent the cryptocurrency that is being used for transactions.

Let us say that Andy wants to send money to Brenda, in this case 10 CRTC. Currently the ledger shows that Andy has 5o units, and Brenda, 10. He broadcasts the message to the network that says,

"Send 10 CRTC from Andy to Brenda."

The transaction will broadcast the information to all the nodes in the system:

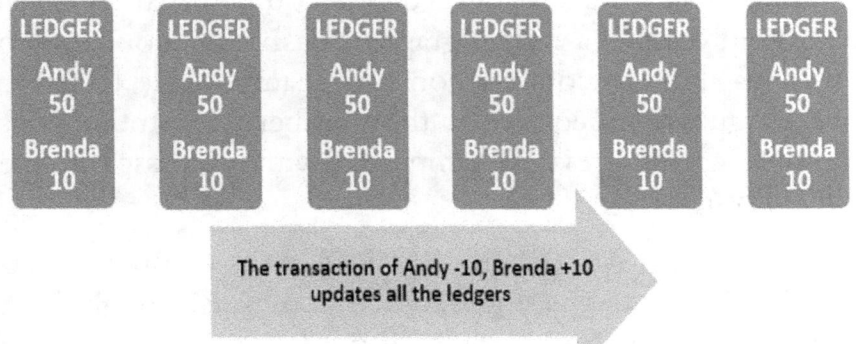

Everyone on the network who wishes to maintain the system, will get a copy of transaction, and pass the transaction information on to other nodes in the system.

This ledger system sounds a pretty similar to the way any bank keeps a ledger. In this case, instead a single entity maintaining the ledger like a bank, a group of several nodes maintain the ledger and everyone in the CTRC network knows about each other's transactions. When the bank maintains the ledgers in a typical banking transaction, they are the "trusted party" in the whole system.

Each node who receives the initial broadcast will update their copy of the ledger and inform others to do the same. The question arises though:

"How can we be sure that Andy and everybody else recorded the transaction correctly?"

The solution is that the CRTC protocol requires a highly complicated form of password, called a digital signature, which is required for EACH transaction. As in a handwritten signature on a paper document, it provides the validity of the broadcasted transaction, but instead of a physical signature, the authenticity is accomplished via a complex mathematical algorithm called a cryptographic hash function, which creates a number combination that is impossible to figure out by guessing because of the number of combinations possible. This prevents tampering with addresses in the CRTC system.

For example, if Andy sends 10 CRTC units to Brenda, and 20 CRTC units to Cal, the transaction messages might look like the following (but in digital format):

> Andy to Brenda – 10 CRTC units, Digital signature :
>
> Andy to Cal   –20 CRTC units, Digital signature :

Why is this digital signature so special? Because of the impossibility of faking or tampering with a transaction. First, there are two components to this signature/password: a PRIVATE KEY and a PUBLIC KEY. The system for broadcasting digital signatures looks like this:

> To create the transaction, a PRIVATE KEY + MESSAGES creates a signature.

Therefore to "spend" money, you have to prove that Andy is the real owner of a public key address to where the funds was sent. This is symbolized the following cryptographic function (f is the function that generates the signature):

> SIGNATURE = f (MESSAGE, PRIVATE KEY)

To verify that Andy is the owner of the public key, the cryptocurrency network will take the digital signature together with another message in a different function to verify that it corresponds with Andy's public key, where v is the verification function:

v(message, public key, SIGNATURE)

The private key is Andy's own personal key for the transaction, while the public key is used by others to check it. The public key is the "send to" address, so when Andy sends Brenda 10 CRTC, he is really sending it to Brenda's public key. Note that these keys ARE IMBEDDED cryptographically within a string of characters that contain the messages and signature so it is impossible to figure them out.

A private key is generated by "key generation" programs. Some of these are resident in CRTC wallets (We will discuss wallets in more detail in Chapter 7).

An example of private key generated is:

2CF24DBA5FB0A30E26E83B2AC5B9E29E1B161E5C1F A7425E73043362938B9824

For example, in Bitcoin, a private wallet generator would look like the following:

1427L1ARMZ2AP2oHdUhwY9vuLCfGqfgX2u 10 CRTC
➔ 15IJkaap9wkCnaUoXuwCxFLeXAtoW4C4

By a complicated mathematical algorithm behind the DIGITAL SIGNATURE, the nodes are able to check if Andy actually owned a private key, without actually seeing the private key because it is buried within the verification message. While the private key can be considered as the true password, the signature together with the private messages proves that Andy possesses the password without telling people what the private key is.

Because the math combines both the private key and a unique message, the password will be different for each transaction and cannot be used again by anyone else for another transaction. No one can also change the message as it passes through the network because any change in the message will nullify the signature, because the fraudulent or erroneous message will not agree with the thousands of other users who are processing the message. This is the Byzantine General problem solution in action!

The math behind creating the signature is really complex, and the signatures generated are comprised of numbers and letters that cannot be duplicated or tampered with because of the impossible levels of probability. For example, just for a private key, there can be 2 to the 256th possible combinations for a key. To drive this point home, 2 to the 40th power is 1,000,995,116,000. That is trillions; and to get to 2 to the 256th, multiply that number by and its products by two <u>216 more times</u>. The resulting number will nave close to 100 zeroes.

And what is the chances that Andy can send to a duplicate address or conversely, Brenda getting the same transaction from a duplicate address? Let us look at a mind boggling analogy as to the number of addresses. It is estimated that the total grains of sand on earth totals around 10,000,000,000,000,000,000. The total number of possible number CTRC addresses is equal to each of the 10,000,000,000,000,000,000 grains of sands having ANOTHER ENTIRE PLANET of the same number of grains of sand! If you ever figure out what that number is, it is still much smaller than the total number of total CTRC addresses.

Assurance of transactions' accuracy and adequacy of funds

We have seen how digital signatures work to make sure that each transaction is authorized and cannot be tampered with. But if Andy sends 10 CRTC to Brenda, how can the system be sure that Andy actually has the money to spend? Does Andy have money to pay? While a typical bank ledger would contain the balance of Andy's account if he had money in the bank, THERE ARE NO RECORDS OF ACCOUNT BALANCES at all in a cryptocurrency system.

Instead of balances, however, the ownership of CRTC is verified by different links to Andy's previous transactions.

To send the 10 CRTC to Brenda, Andy has to refer to previous transactions where he received at least 10 CRTC's. The CRTC system doesn't care how much money Andy has, it only cares whether he has 10 CRTC at the very moment that he transmits money to Brenda. These previous transactions referred to are called INPUTS. The other nodes in the CRTC network will verify these inputs to ensure that Andy was truly the recipient of money, and that these previous inputs total 10 or more CRTCs.

Let us see an example of this in action. The following ledger shows the INPUT data which tells us that Andy has more than enough of previous transactions to pay for the 10 CRTCs that he is sending to Brenda.

ANDY'S INPUT TRANSACTIONS					
Previous Output	Amount	From address	Type	Script Sig
gh825usw1-1	1.1	sdfFJDfd4538J	Address	1e21f77tpiaebhsmk6ce
nw97u6ttb-a	2.4	m4BlKRpsQynA	Address	4rrw7gmz0dbispwjjwx5
4t89jmsoi-b	0.5	71fSZMoPGSS5	Address	q9ejzxo9y8v496dn43sh
Tsabkumaa-x	6.0	CQYbIbPiev8P	Address	papeqv7ld5z9n7dcenz3
k2dco5yoh-m	.8	mfEeEECC0A6S	Address	p5lghttvmadlyzaqp8pa

TOTAL: 11.3 (Enough to cover his transactions)

The CRTC system therefore, adds up the total INPUTS until it finds out that Andy has sufficient (at least 10 CRTC units) to pay Brenda.

The digital transactions that will be sent back to send 10 CRTCs to Brenda's account is called OUTPUT. Output actually, might have two components. One is sending the money to Brenda, and the other is sending change back to Andy just in case previous INPUTS exceed 10 CRTCs.

We can see that the ownership of CRTC is passed from one person to another via some kind of chain. Each transaction that that is processed is always dependent on previous transactions. To make sure that the nodes can trust the transactions that led to Andy's 10 CRTC's, the nodes' wallets will download all the transactions that were ever made and will check each of the transactions' validity from the VERY BEGINNING! It is very important for a wallet to validate these transactions especially since the CRTC system is populated by complete strangers.

The Double Spending Issue – the time factor

To summarize CRTC security, we can see that when the other system users verify the Digital Signature, only Andy could have created the transaction message "sending" money to Brenda. To make sure that Andy has enough funds to send Brenda, the users also check every past transaction referenced as input, to make sure that what Andy is sending Brenda is unspent.

There is still one hole that needs to be plugged in the CRTC system, and that is to prevent users like Andy from using the same money twice, by sending the same transaction one after another. If Andy only had 10 CRTC units to begin with, he could place two orders and receive both orders before the CRTC has time to check them:

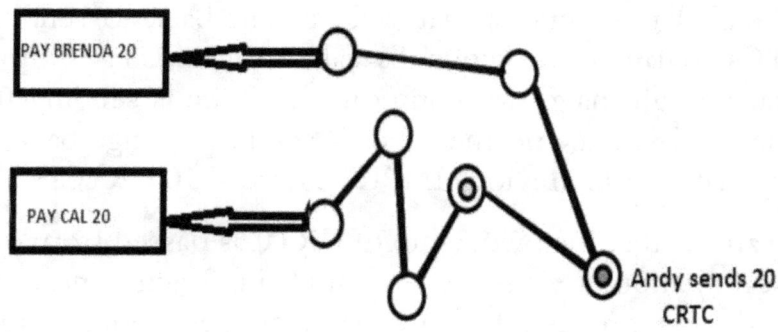

Because the transactions are passed along to each and every node in the CRTC system, the order in which they are received is the same as the order when they were created. Even so-called "timestamps" cannot be trusted because Andy could easily misrepresent the transaction time. Because there is no central computer to check the time, like a credit card or a bank system, there is no way to verify the correct chronological sequence.

Fraud is therefore possible because Andy can now wait for Brenda to ship her product, and then send another payment transaction to Cal, or even to himself using the same input references. If she is really unlucky, Brenda would have shipped the product and not get any money because Cal or even Andy would have gotten it first.

The solution to this is a "mathematical race" incorporated in the bedrock of a cryptocurrency system: The blockchain.

Chapter 5

Blockchains and Mining – the Key to Cryptocurrency

Definition

A cryptocurrency system relies on a key component called a blockchain, and these two terms have sometimes been used interchangeably. The blockchain, which we will be describing in detail in this chapter, is the underlying protocol that allows for the transfer of cryptocurrency and ensures a bulletproof transaction verification system to avoid fraud and malice. It is the most significant and powerful development in cryptocurrency technology. The power of this technology also lies in its capability in distributing information across all the individual computers (called nodes) within the system. The term blockchain has often been interchanged with distributed ledger technology.

The advantage of blockchain is it is distributed across all the nodes in the system. A particular cryptocurrency's blockchain database does not exist in a single location or is under the control of a single central authority, but exists or is hosted by thousands of computers at any single time.

The blockchain network contains a self-review or auditing system that because of the thousands of users confirming transactions, practically guarantee the accuracy and integrity of transactions and data residing in its ledgers. This security feature of a blockchain system is mostly brought about by the cryptographic manipulation and verification of data making it mathematically improbable to manipulate, change, and duplicate transactions. Not even massive computer power can hope to disrupt the blockchain system.

Blockchains are composed of three core parts:

The Block: This is simply transactions that are listed in a ledger over time. The amount, the time period, the number of transactions, and the even that triggered the creation of the block (payment, transfer, receipt) is different for each block. It would look like the following, non-digitally:

Chain: Every block contains a hash of the previous block that "chained" it to the previous one. A computed hash successfully computed by a node mathematically links the block to another block. This concept is one of the most complex and difficult ones to understand in the cryptocurrency system, because it requires the use of fairly advanced arithmetic. But the chain is the glue magic that links the blocks together and provides the system of mathematical "trust" where no other trust exists in the cryptographic universe.

Hash: A very unique mathematical "signature" that is created from the information in a preceding block. Consider the hash as a unique fingerprint that solidly locks in the blocks together in time and order. Cryptograhic hashing which creates the hash, was invented many decades ago, and was incorporated into cryptocurrency systems to provide unique identifiers for their transactions. This was the only "out" that the founders of cryptocurrency system saw that could replace the trust function of traditional currency and monetary systems.

Hashing generates a one-way mechanism which cannot be decrypted by creating a mathematical algorithm that orders data of a specified size and reducing it to a string of bits with a fixed size. The typical bit is about thirty two characters long. This string is a numerical representation of the data in the blockchain that was just "hashed" or encrypted.

A quick note on the math used in cryptocurrencies: Bitcoin uses the Secure Hash Algorithm (SHA) as a cryptographic hash functions used in its blockchains. It is a one of the most widely known algorithms and creates a unique, fixed-size 256-bit (32-byte) fixed-size hash.

<u>Network</u>: The network is comprised of "full nodes." Together they function as a single mechanism running an algorithm that secures the network. Each node will have a complete record of all the transactions that were ever recorded in that blockchain.

The advantage of blockchain is it is distributed across all the nodes in the system. A particular cryptocurrency's blockchain database does not exist in a single location or is under the control of a single central authority, but exists or is hosted by thousands of computers at any single time.

The blockchain network contains a self-review or auditing system that because of the thousands of users confirming transactions, practically guarantee the accuracy and integrity of transactions and data residing in its ledgers. This security feature of a blockchain system is mostly brought about by the cryptographic manipulation and verification of data making it mathematically improbable to manipulate, change, and duplicate transactions. Not even massive computer power can hope to disrupt the blockchain system.

Proper ordering

To start the blockchain process, Andy's transaction is placed in correct order by including his transaction in a block together with a group of other transactions. It then eventually links them in the block chain after the fulfillment of a set of conditions.

Do not confuse this with the transactions to determine if Andy had enough CRTC to be able to pay Brenda. Those transactions tracked how Andy accumulated ownership of CRTC, while the block chain is used to put transactions in order:

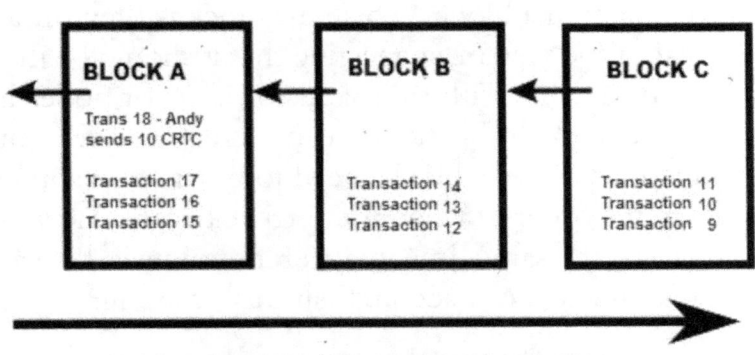

Note from the above diagram that every block references the past immediate block, placing the blocks in chronological order. It is possible to go back all the way back in time to reference the very first block of transactions ever made. Transactions in Block A, where Andy's transaction is, happened at the same time, while transactions not yet grouped in a block are "unconfirmed" or "unordered":

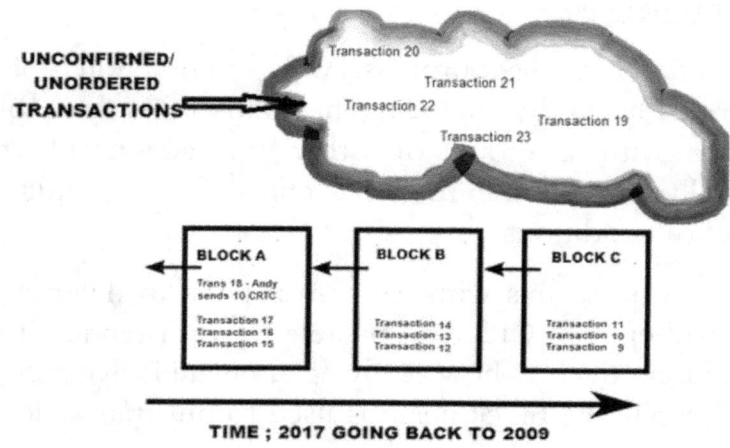

Any user can accumulate a set of unordered transactions and assemble them in a block. This new block is then broadcast to the rest of the system, suggesting that it should be the next block in the chain. With thousands of users or nodes in the system, several of them can create new blocks simultaneously. These blocks need to be ordered somehow, and not in the order of when they arrive, because new blocks can appear at the same time in different points in the system. How does the network accomplish this ordering?

Mathematical puzzles and miners

The solution is that a contest now ensues where a valid block should contain the solution to a complex mathematical problem. The nodes' computers run the entire block text of through random guessing programs called a

CRYPTOGRAPHIC HASH until it arrives at at the correct answer. We will not go into the mathematical detail of the "hashing" because of the lengthy explanation that might appeal to a mathematics oriented few.

All we need to know is that the solution to the problem is totally unpredictable, and the only way to get the correct answer is through random guesses. Because of the hashing requirements and the extremely high number of possibilities, it takes several years of manual guessing to get to the right answer. In the cryptocurrency system, since there are thousands of computers working 24/7, it takes an average of about 10 minutes for a correct solution to come up, meaning that a new block is "chained" to the block chain every ten minutes.

The first node or person to solve the problem will then broadcast their "winning" block and this block of transactions is now accepted as the next block in the chain. The extreme randomness in the complex problem makes it unlikely for two or more people to arrive at the solution at the same time. Unlikely however, does not mean never, and occasionally two blocks will be solved at the same time. The system will have a "tie-breaker" system that involves the ultimate winning node to have solved another problem and determining who the winner is by how much transactions they have in their blocks.

The block is finally created after tremendous work using powerful computers engaging in what is essentially a shoot and miss trial-and-error computational exercise. A "miner" will finally emerge with the one block hash containing the cryptocurrency algorithm was waiting and looking for – a mathematical answer with the exact number of zeros required together with various other conditions.

The mathematical puzzles are so complex and difficult, that users are sure that it is impossible for an "attacker" to come in and insert bogus answers to the blockchain problems. Nodes trust the cryptocurrency protocol to protect users from such invaders, but no trust is required among the users.

With tens of thousands of miners working continuously, we have seen that nothing in the processes that we have described requires trust between the people working the problems. If anything, miners want other miners to fail in their cryptographic work so that they can get to add a new block to the chain first, and collect their cryptocurrency payment.

To read more about blockchain order my other book now available

Blockchain - Learn Block Chain Technology Quickly

What you need to know in an hour

Chapter 6

Putting it all together – Mining, buying and selling with cryptocurrency

With knowledge of the inner workings of blockchain technology, we will now turn to how people acquire, sell, and enter into various cryptocurrencies and how they are used in real-world commerce.

The granddaddy of cryptocurrency, Bitcoin has often been mentioned interchangeably with cryptocurrency itself. As of July 31, 2017, there were about 16 million Bitcoin in circulation with a market value of almost 70 billion U.S. dollars. The "top 100" cryptocurrencies have a market value of over 150 billion USD. This amount of purchasing power is pretty substantial and cryptocurrencies are being used with increasing frequency and regularity as more people continue to (1) know about them, (2) appreciate their qualities, and (3) understand how their limitations.

The "mining" reward

When we discussed blockchains in the previous chapter, we saw that they are "completed" by users who are willing to solve mathematical puzzles. After proof of work is established, the first node to get the answer to the math problem broadcasts the "successful" block, which is now accepted as the next block to be linked in the chain. The high number of people trying to solve the puzzles together with the extreme randomness of the math problem makes it practically impossible for two or more people to come up with the correct answer at the same time. In mining, the more hashes are completed, the higher the chances a block can be linked to the block chain, together with the chances of earning cryptocurrency increases.

Nodes are solving for, and computing the cryptographic puzzles all over the world, and anyone with a computer can simply take their shot at it. It can become costly, difficult, and with more and more people trying to solve the cryptographic puzzles every day, more time-consuming and requiring increasing amounts of computer power. Unless someone is just trying to have fun solving complex algorithms, they do it with a reward in mind. Those who do this dirty digital digging are called "miners".

The cryptocurrency ecosystem incentivizes miners by rewarding them with tokens and cryptocurrency units every time they solve a blockchain. The cryptocurrency algorithm rewards them for essentially providing a service for all users of the network. This effort is done either individually or by mining pools.

Mining for cryptocurrency

If you are really up to the investment of time and money, you need to purchase the requisite hardware and software for the effort. In the "good old days" (really just about five years ago), you could get by with just an above average CPU to do the hash work and the cryptography required to complete block chains. Specialized hardware and accessories in the market today are available from $5,000 USD and up.

You also need to have the proper software to help you mine cryptocurrency. Many of these can be downloaded for free, while some products will require either a purchase or subscription for their supposed "extra features" to help you along. Cryptocurrency mining software are supposed to do the highly complex perform complex hash calculations, towards solving the mathematical puzzles.

Many people have entered into cryptocurrency mining full-time, and the effort not only includes putting money, but also keeping up to date with the latest news and developments. With computer technology moving forward at the rate that it is, serious miners cannot afford to be left behind.

<u>Mining pools</u>

"Solo mining" is either too time consuming and/or expensive for some people. Instead, they join mining pools to help increase their chances of getting cryptocurrency. Special equipment and software is used whether cryptocurrency is mined individually or in pools. In mining pools, members get shares of cryptocurrency earned for "successful" hashes.

While the share an individual gets from a successfully linked block chain (or solved puzzle) is smaller than if an individual mined it, the chances of success are increased when more people work on the blocks.

<u>Getting and earning cryptocurrency the "easy" way</u>

If you don't want to spend the time, money, and computing power to mine for bitcoin, a much easier way to get or earn cryptocurrency is to sell goods and services and tell people that you are using cryptocurrency. Most vendors who accept cryptocurrency seem to take only Bitcoin, but a growing number of cryptocurrency are gaining the necessary reputation to gain wider acceptance.

A good first step to earning cryptocurrency is to sell merchandise on Ebay or be a registered vendor in online marketplaces that accept bitcoin for payment. These are forward looking business enterprises payment systems have been configured to allow for the receipt of Bitcoin for payment. On Ebay for example, Paypal is now equipped to take Bitcoin deposits to be used as payment.

Buying with cryptocurrency

A growing list of companies in the United States, as well as online stores abroad take cryptocurrency especially Bitcoin, as payment. Among the well-known places that accept Bitcoin include: Overstock.com, Microsoft, Subway, Virgin Galactic, travel booking sites Expedia and CheapAir.com, and the gaming portal Zynga. You can also purchase from Gap, GameStop and JC Penney if you use eGifter.com.

Regardless of how you obtain, earn, or spend cryptocurrency, you will need a digital/electronic "wallet" to keep your money in.

Chapter 7

Getting Cryptocurrencies – Wallets and Exchanges

<u>Cryptocurrency digital wallets</u>

For most people, block chain, hashes, and cryptographic algorithms are a bit too much to deal with for those who just want to accumulate cryptocurrencies or use it as currency. No matter how you obtain or use cryptocurrency, you need a digital wallet to house the cryptocurrency in.

You need the wallet to store, receive, and send cryptocurrency unless you have developed a sophisticated method to warehouse it. Most of the coins in circulation such as Bitcoin, Ethereum, and Litecoin actually have "official" wallets, or they recommend third party ones that conform to their particular cryptocurrency.

Unlike typical physical wallets, digital wallets do not actually contain or store cryptocurrency. In Chapter 3, we discussed how cryptocurrency systems are all about maintaining transaction ledgers and simply add and subtract the amounts of your total cryptocurrency transactions and determine how much your "balance" is. In fact, the most important "item" stored in a digital wallet is the private and public keys that we discussed earlier. A reputable wallet will store a personal ledger of transactions involving your personal accounts.

The digital wallet will allow anyone to perform electronic transactions which includes online purchases and sales. A digital wallet also allows an owner to link a bank account with the wallet. This can be useful if there is a desire to purchase or sell cryptocurrency and using regular dollars to purchase or sell them. Some wallets even allow for the storage of identification cards like insurance or health cards, drivers licenses, membership cards, loyalty cards and others. These credentials can then be transmitted wirelessly to a merchant terminal by using Near Field Communication, or NFC technology. In NFC, the phone is simply placed again a reader to complete a transaction.

In effect, digital wallets not only allow purchase and sale transactions but also related authentication processes to validated personal credentials. For example, the digital wallet can be used to validate someone using cryptocurrency to buy alcohol with the wallet owner's credentials that contain his age.

The best feature of the wallet is that the validation work that is conducted by the system to verify transactions, hashes, addresses, etc. are done in the background and is simply picked up by the wallet as transactions to be read and included in your history.

There are hundreds of digital wallet platforms available today, and the more prominent ones, like Coinbase and Mycelium are all free to join, have good reputations, and are pretty easy to sign up for. After using Google Play or the Itunes store to install the wallet app, the user only needs to enter very little pertinent information. Aside from an e-mail address, no other personal information is required. Sales and purchases are practically single click transactions. If the user has previous bitcoin transactions, these will be located when the system locates the private key that the user has been using.

Wallet security

While cryptocurrency wallets are designed to be secure and generally anonymous, security actually varies from one wallet to another. Ultimately, just a regular physical wallet or any other (non-cryptocurrency) digital wallet, the safety and security will depend on common sense practices. Many serious users maintain more than one wallet, using each separate wallet for different reasons. Added security layers include the encryption of the wallet, the use of something like a Google authenticator, or the use of multi-signature transactions.

It is also a good idea to back up the "contents" of a wallet, especially the private keys. Contents can be used typical backup systems like a thumb drive or portable hard drive. As to privacy and anonymity, the obvious answer is you should not put any specific identifying marks on your wallet via your private key or your login name. The cryptocurrency ecosystem is public and open source in nature with the blockchain ledgers being subject to scrutiny by everyone. It is possible to reverse engineer information to identify someone specifically, but it would be an extremely difficult process. If you are smart and try to leave as inconspicuous a footprint as possible, it is almost a lock that you will be anonymous during your existence in the cryptocurrency universe.

Which wallet?

There are many "brands" of digital wallets in the cryptocurrency ecosystem that advertise their own supposedly wonderful features and advantages. But no matter what that brand is, All wallets should be able to allow a user to access their information on a hand held gadget, desktop, or laptop. The following are the types of wallets available:

Mobile – Run from an app that can be used on your smartphone or tablet.

Desktop – Run from a desktop application that is connected to a cryptocurrency system directly. Desktops and mobile devices are the most common forms of a digital wallet.

Hardware – These are devices that are dedicated to "hold" cryptocurrency transaction information and keep it secure. This can be in the form of USB devices for example and can connect online to access the cryptocurrency system.

Online - This wallet is essentially web-based, where the information is available on a server.

Paper - A QR code is printed for the private and public keys. This option allows someone to not store any digital data or leave any form of identity online.

A word of caution: Regardless of the form you choose as your cryptocurrency wallet, if you lose or misplace your private key, you will lose your "money". If you lose your cryptocurrency because you lost your key, you are out of luck.

Cryptocurrency exchanges

Parties interested in publicly trading in stocks have the New York Stock Exchange and NASDAQ, and those who want to publicly buy and sell practically everything else has the Chicago Mercantile Exchange. These exchanges locate and link together buyers and sellers of financial instruments (including currency), and post current market prices to guide the parties interested in trading. There are no such mega exchanges that deal with cryptocurrency as of the present.

While no such facility yet exists for cryptocurrency, there are many public exchanges on websites where people can buy, sell, trade, and even exchange cryptocurrencies not only for conventional fiat currency like U.S. dollars and the Euro, but also for other cryptocurrency issues. Someone wanting to trade in Bitcoin using Litecoin can google "cryptocurrency exchanges" to see what outfits are engaged in public trading.

These exchanges are all private businesses and are not generally subject to any regulatory oversight by any country's government. A lot of them are also based outside the United States, so extreme care must be taken before considering them. Some exchanges offer themselves to more "advanced" traders, by allowing for the execution of highly specialized and esoteric transactions like liquidity swaps. They may also allow for short-selling and margin trading. It is important to note that most of them have been around for less than ten years, so their stability and reputation are not yet quite tested.

People can use some exchanges on a one-time basis, without having to provide too much information to register, such as providing addresses and social security numbers. Others who want to trade full-time and "professionally" will likely need to provide multiple identification and will be required to open an account.

There are three basic kinds of cryptocurrency exchanges:

Direct Trades – In these platforms, people meet directly with other parties from other countries to exchange currencies. The parties agree on a price or exchange rate.

Trade Platforms – Buyers and sellers are connected through what is essentially a website "meeting place". The website owner where the trading parties connect take a fee from each transaction.

Brokerages - These are websites where any interested party can by cryptocurrencies at prices set at the brokerage. These function essentially as money changers in the real currency markets.

As in anything else that requires an outlay of money, some preparatory work should be done before joining an exchange, much less part with hard-earned money. The following are what prospective investors and traders should consider:

Reputation – Unlike exchanges of traditional financial and commercial products, cryptocurrency exchanges have not been around for a very long time. The ideal way to find out about the integrity of an exchange is through third party testimonies and personal experiences of others. With the explosion of cryptocurrency, there are many online discussion forums where exchanges are discussed and even rated.

Fees and charges - A reputable exchange will disclose what their fees are up front. A prospective customer should know what charges and fees are for different transactions, such as transfers, payments, and even receipts. It pays to compare fees not only as absolute amounts, but also consider the quality, speed, and transparency of the services rendered.

Funding and payment - It is important that an exchange offers multiple ways to allow someone to transfer funds in and out of an exchange. There are a variety of ways that money can flow in and out: Debit cards, direct debits of bank accounts, wire transfers, PayPal, and even credit cards. Wire transfers usually require a lot of documentation up front, while credit card transactions will usually demand sufficient identification before a transaction is approved. Privacy and security can be compromised if the exchange has limited funding options.

Most trading platforms in the United States and the U.K. will ask for government-issued I.D. before they allow withdrawals and deposits. Some of these verification procedures can take days, but they exist to protect everyone from problems in dealing with what is essentially an unregulated financial instrument. There are other exchanges outside those countries' jurisdictions however, that will allow traders to keep their anonymity.

Some foreign exchanges may have restrictions if transactions are done of the United States or other Western European countries. Other countries' looser regulatory structures may run afoul of reporting requirements in the U.S. It is important to consider what functions and tools are allowable and legal across international borders.

Exchange rates – When using an exchange domiciled in other countries, exchanging cryptocurrency for U.S. dollars may require not only a fee, but also a steep foreign exchange conversion difference. Rate fluctuations and fees can sometimes be up to 10% of the total transaction value. Once again it pays to shop around for more favorable foreign exchange policies.

Chapter 8

The Future of Cryptocurrency

You can walk into Helen's Pizza store in Bergen New Jersey without any cash, credit, or debit card and still fill yourself up with a pepperoni slice and a soda. To pay for your meal, you point your phone at a sign beside the cash register and in an instant, you have paid for your meal using cryptocurrency, in this case, Bitcoin. If pizza is not your thing, you can walk a few blocks and get a sub at a Subway location and pay digitally as well.

You can also pay using cryptocurrency for travel (Expedia and Virgin), merchandise (Overstock.com), and for software from Microsoft. Microsoft founder Bill Gates is a supporter of cryptocurrency and thinks that it is a electronic revolution of tsunami proportions that cannot be avoided, but needs to be embraced and accepted.

The popularity of cryptocurrency has increased on a logarithmic scale ever since it became a public medium of exchange less than ten years ago. The very first Bitcoin released in 2009 had a value of less than a penny with just a few thousand being issued by the founders. Not a single commercial transaction occurred using Bitcoin until 2010. One of the first transactions, which became widely famous was the issuance of 10,000 Bitcoin units to purchase $25 worth of pizza.

This means that at the time, Bitcoin was valued at only $.0025 per unit. By the middle of 2017, the average monthly Bitcoin volume was over $60 billion dollars representing almost 2,000,000 transactions. Probably the most astounding statistic that a Bitcoin unit as of the end of July, 2017 is valued at around $4,000. This means that if you bought $10.00 worth of Bitcoin in 2009, that "portfolio" would be worth $50 million today!

But outside of Bitcoin, the cryptocurrency market is also exploding. With over seven hundred systems available, paying using this new digital currency is becoming more widespread. The scale of the use of currency is either alarming or promising, depending on one's viewpoint.

And while cryptocurrency is not yet traded on any major commodity exchange, the New York Stock Exchange in 2015 began posting bitcoin price index with the symbol NYXBT, a major acknowledgement not only of the existence of cryptocurrency, but also of its growing notoriety and use. The NYXBT price is posted every afternoon and also published at the exchange's Global Index Feed, or GIF. Cryptocurrency has grown way beyond being anonymous and staying under the radar, and both its currency value and use are growing.

Total cryptocurrency in circulation is just below 9% of total U.S. dollar currency in circulation. This means that almost 1 out of 10 transaction dollars is made in cryptocurrency. Bitcoin are mostly used in transactions using smart phones, and with a big percentage of people now doing their commerce on portable gadgets, cryptocurrency's share of total business transactions is expected to increase. To what extent this will happen largely depends on how reliable in continues to be in providing anonymity and rock solid mathematical soundness.

Through July 31, 2017, cryptocurrency use is legal in most countries, which means that currencies such as Bitcoin can be used to buy or sell goods and services. There are very few countries where cryptocurrency is illegal. What clouds the legality issue is that a unit of cryptocurrency itself cannot be bought or sold in some countries. As more people in the less "stable" nations begin to appreciate and know about cryptocurrency, they can begin comparing it to their own sovereign currencies and may conclude that stability-wise, what their central banks circulate is not as attractive as cryptocurrency.

There are financial executives in the United States who are also trying to incorporate cryptocurrencies in other financial instruments such as derivatives and exchange traded funds. While there are the expected bumps in the road with the Securities and Exchange Commission and other agencies, the momentum to move cryptocurrency beyond its current reputation as an underground currency for nerds seems to be building.

With blockchain technology being considered in other applications, its growing reputation can only add to the viability and reliability of cryptocurrency. For example, there is a growing interest in "smart contracts," where computer protocols can execute and complete the provisions of a contract without requiring a trusted third party to verify and validate them.

The growing interest towards block chain applications has put the spotlight on cryptocurrency, because it is the first ostensibly successful application of the technology applied universally. The gatekeepers of the cryptocurrency world will be best served to make sure their ecosystem survives and thrives.

Conclusion

Cryptocurrency is not the next big investment technology, It has already arrived!.. It needs to be accepted and respected as a new way of doing business, and one that is done by not just regular people, but by a class of people considered smarter than the rest of the general population. User profiles suggest that a majority of cryptocurrency users are highly educated and computer literate.

For all its promises, however, there some serious concerns about their use and their long-term viability.

Because of its anonymity, many people tend to use it for nefarious purposes. On the dark web, you can purchase illegal goods and services with Bitcoin and other cryptocurrencies. There have been some highly publicized arrests over the use of some of the purchases, and while the perpetrators and the dark web were the focus, cryptocurrency was the secondary character in the legal and law enforcement scenarios that unfolded. The danger with bad press is not just that cryptocurrency may lose its appeal and value with regular users. A bigger danger to cryptocurrency viability is that that sovereign governments may decide to shut down a cryptocurrency system if its use violates national interests.

The other issue that will be interesting to watch will be how the system protocol for Bitcoin will adjust to "compensate" miners when Bitcoin issuance ceases in 2041. Miners get "paid" by being awarded Bitcoin for linking blockchains. Because miners verify and validate transactions, they are essential to the survival and operation to the cryptocurrency system. Since they will no longer be able to mine for bitcoins, will the system protocol instead pay them a fee? If so, in what form will this compensation take?

A much talked (complained?) about downside in cryptocurrency systems is the lack of fallback or insurance in case you lose your private key, or if somehow your cryptocurrency disappears into thin air. More than anything else, this is what keeps a big number of people from even thinking of jumping into the cryptocurrency waters. With a Bitcoin unit trading near $5,000, it is a big commitment to trust something that has no physical presence, with no guarantee against loss due to negligence or fraud. As this "no central authority" trust system is central to the cryptocurrency model, insurance and a 1-800 customer support number is not likely to be available.

Computer power requirements also represents another potential risk and disadvantage of the cryptocurrency system. In the unlikely event that a catastrophic event wipes out power and electricity over an extended period of time, commercial activity around a cryptocurrency will come to a halt. People will not have any physical currency to pull out of their pockets to pay for goods and services. Whatever purchasing power or monetary assets in a cryptocurrency system are essentially useless and non-existent in a world without adequate computing power and worse, with no computing power at all.

Ultimately however, we are in the digital age and cryptocurrency by definition, is digital currency. If we are to keep up with the times, our financial systems need to keep up with the digitization of the rest of our lives.

Cryptocurrency is quickly emerging from the depths of algorithmic mystery as just some form of shadow currency. While you may not yet buy your first unit of cryptocurrency after reading my book, I trust that you now know more than you need than just a surface grasp of its concepts.

I hope this book is able to help you to get a working knowledge of cryptocurrencies and their underlying systems and trust that you are now ready to apply everything you have learned from this book (if you have not done so already).

Finally, if you enjoyed this book, then I'd like to ask you for a favor, would you be kind enough to leave a review for this book on Amazon? It'd be greatly appreciated!

Click here to leave a review for this book on Amazon!

Thank you and good luck!

Preview Of 'Blockchain–Learn Blockchain Quickly. What you need to know in an hour'

A blockchain, on a surface level, functions like the Google spreadsheet that you may use on a regular basis – people can write on it, and you can keep track of all the changes that are made among the users who has the permission to edit it. You may think of your spreadsheet as a very important tool that keeps all your data in check and can be updated on a regular basis.

Today, most of the transactions that you do daily is stored on a company's database – your online purchases, social media entries, blog uploads, etc. needs to be kept in a secure server so that you can keep track of what's happening to them. However, you know that the world is not a perfect place. It is always possible for a server to go down, crippling thousands or even millions of online consumers that will not be able to access a data or service that they need. It is also possible for irregularities to happen in-between transaction. That makes every consumer want a system that they can easily check and would be secure enough for all their transactions to never be tampered with for anyone's gain.

The blockchain technology promises to do all that by keeping a decentralized ledger of transactions that allows everyone access for the right checks and balances. When implemented across industries, this technology will change the way you think about security and transparency.

To read more about blockchain technology order my other book now available.

Blockchain - Learn Block Chain Technology Quickly

What you need to know in an hour

www.ingramcontent.com/pod-product-compliance
Lightning Source LLC
Chambersburg PA
CBHW071548240526
45470CB00023B/2074